SKILLS FOR SUCCESS™

STRENGTHENING RESEARCH PAPER SKILLS

PHILIP WOLNY

Rosen
YA™

New York

Published in 2018 by The Rosen Publishing Group, Inc.
29 East 21st Street, New York, NY 10010

First Edition

Library of Congress Cataloging-in-Publication Data

Names: Wolny, Philip, author.
Title: Strengthening research paper skills / Philip Wolny.
Description: New York : Rosen Publishing, 2018. | Series: Skills for success | Includes bibliographical references and index. | Audience: Grade 7–12.
Identifiers: ISBN 9781508175728 (library bound)
Subjects: LCSH: Report writing—Juvenile literature. | Research—Juvenile literature.
Classification: LCC LB1047.3 W65 2018 | DDC 371.30281—dc23

Manufactured in the United States of America

CONTENTS

Introduction 4

CHAPTER ONE
Research Paper: A Definition................................7

CHAPTER TWO
Where to Begin 14

CHAPTER THREE
Doing the Research 21

CHAPTER FOUR
Organize, Outline, Write, and Edit........................31

CHAPTER FIVE
Research Citations and Ethics.............................39

CHAPTER SIX
Research into Your Future 45

Glossary 53

For More Information 55

For Further Reading...58

Bibliography 59

Index...61

INTRODUCTION

A student will write many different kinds of papers throughout his or her school years. One of the most important types of papers teachers ask for is the research paper. You can bet that at some point from high school and beyond—especially when moving on to college or university and graduate school—that you will have to write one.

The first couple of times one attempts to write a research paper the task can seem overwhelming. This is partly because it may require more work than one has had to do before and also because research papers demand higher standards. Personal essays, stories, book reports, and similar assignments students receive early in their school careers are more or less straightforward. Students must think carefully beforehand about how to prepare for research papers and write them in a formal, professional way.

Say, for instance, that a history teacher assigns a topic to research and write about. The argument you have to make is that the rise of the internet since the 1990s has had an impact on a rise or fall in childhood literacy rates. Or, imagine you are assigned to figure out if banning advertisements for alcohol and tobacco products has decreased rates of smoking and alcohol use among minors and

As with any skill, you can learn how to write research papers by approaching the task methodically. After a few attempts, it will feel like it's second nature.

young people. What questions should you first ask yourself? What will your approach be? Where do you begin? It is natural to panic when you are assigned something new and complicated.

There's no need to just sit there and worry, however. Whenever you have a big task to accomplish, a great way to make it manageable is to break everything down into smaller steps and plan ahead. Writing a research paper requires certain skills, and a young writer has to learn them eventually.

In this resource, readers will learn what, exactly, a research paper is, how to start one, what sources are, and how to organize and present their findings in a clear, straightforward way. They will also learn or get a refresher course on how to cite their research sources and how to avoid intentional and even accidental plagiarism.

Many of the skills involved are ones readers will probably already be familiar with. Doing research will strengthen them and give them the necessary tools and confidence to complete stellar research projects. Sharpening your skills now will make your academic life easier throughout your career.

Research has always been important for the sciences, professional academic fields, and in many jobs. In the modern-day information economy, it has become more important than ever. Whether a student is going to become a lawyer, marketing executive, entrepreneur, college professor, member of the military, salesperson, or embark on dozens of other possible career paths, doing good research will always make for a highly useful and well compensated skill set. In addition to the concrete payoffs, doing research helps students learn how to ask questions, organize their own thoughts, and even change their preconceived opinions on certain topics and pressing issues of the day. Let's get started and strengthen our research skills!

chapter ONE

Research Paper: A Definition

Before refining and improving one's research skills, it is necessary to define what, exactly, is to be done. On the surface, it may seem that researching and writing is simple and straightforward. What is so hard about looking up facts and figures online and reporting back what you found? If it sounds deceptively simple, it is actually not. What is a research paper, really?

A research paper is more than just a bunch of information from various sources. It should analyze a perspective or argue a point. It goes beyond simply documenting one's own opinion, though. Instead, one collects information, data, perspectives, and other source content from periodicals, academic articles, books, and both online and physical sources. These sources, along with one's own original thoughts and ideas, are the backbone of research.

A good research paper will make use of the convenient online tools enjoyed by modern scholars but also explore all relevant sources. These can include physical books from school and academic libraries and the various digital and

A well-rounded research effort will include plenty of reading. One goal is to cover information and ideas that may be new to you.

physical records libraries maintain. Many of these are still not accessible with merely a standard internet connection.

On a basic level, a research paper is an essay, but an expanded one. A high school research paper may be relatively short—only ten typed pages, for example. A higher-level research paper for college or graduate school is often dozens of pages long and can even reach into the triple digits.

Looking around online, you may notice that you can find reports released by various national or international organizations, some of them hundreds of pages long. For instance, check out the reports of certain nongovernmental organizations (NGOs), such as Human Rights Watch (HRW) or the World Health Organization (WHO). Note that these research reports can also have many, even hundreds, of contributors. But don't worry: you probably will not ever have to write something so long, unless you really want to. Longer research reports are not usually assigned until students have reached college. By then, you will have become an expert!

BUILDING ON THE WORK OF EXPERTS

One of the key words to remember when approaching a research paper is in the title above, in fact: "expert." According to the online research guidelines from the State University of New York's (SUNY) Empire State College, "When you write a research paper you build upon what you know about the subject and make a deliberate attempt to find out what experts know. A research paper involves surveying a field of knowledge in order to find the best possible information in that field." It is only from expert knowledge, along with information and data that have been confirmed and agreed upon by many experts, that you can obtain the best source material for a research paper.

BEYOND PERSUASION AND OPINION

Another way of looking at research papers is defining what they are not. Personal opinions and beliefs definitely play a role in both doing research and writing a report. They may inspire the ideas for papers to begin with.

But a research paper cannot be strictly an opinion essay or a persuasive essay. You are probably familiar with both kinds and have likely done one or both already. Opinion essays are similar to the opinion editorials, or op-eds, one can find in any newspaper or respected online news source, such as the sites for the *New York Times* or *Bloomberg News.* "Why We Should Abolish the Death Penalty" or "Why We Should Vaccinate Young Children" are examples of titles of possible opinion essays. These kinds of essays take a position on a topic and support that stand with detailed information. Persuasive essays, as the name implies, are written to convince another reader or group of readers to agree with the paper's conclusions. Facts and logic convince the reader.

A research paper would explore these topics differently. For instance, it could examine the death penalty's status among different nations worldwide and its effects on violent crime or public safety. A research report on childhood vaccinations might explore the effects of people's religious views or other personal beliefs on rates of

Articles from newspapers—whether print or online—will figure into many research papers. Remember to read between the lines. That means reading critically.

vaccinations and interpret those connections. The writer's responsibility is to make his or her personal opinions secondary to the objective facts and data the writer uncovers and presents.

ADVANCING KNOWLEDGE, ADVANCING ONESELF

In college and graduate school, students advance in their careers by doing research. To go from a bachelor's degree to a master's degree to a PhD, or doctorate, you must show your research skills and constantly improve them. Research

SURVEYING THE FIELD

For young scholars just learning how to write a research paper, the information revealed in the paper should be new to them. For experienced scholars and those in the private sector, research papers should advance the knowledge in a particular field.

A research paper will often include what some call "surveying the field," that is, a summary of the important historical and current research on a particular subject or question, to provide context. When you are just starting, this kind of review is important. The latest research builds on a long tradition, and all the research, both new and old, makes up what is sometimes known as "the literature" of any given field.

For example, in the field of physics, surveying the field can include a historical rundown of famous figures throughout the history of physics. A survey of economic theories may briefly provide a history and summary of older ideas and then move on to more detailed ones about modern economists and what they believe.

However, there is more to a well-done research paper than writing a survey. Instead, a good research paper will take many of the ideas that might appear in a survey of a field, weigh them, argue for the validity of some and for dropping others, and come to a conclusion of some sort. Hopefully, that conclusion adds something new to the literature.

A research paper about a topic in the biological sciences may rely on laboratory findings, whether they include your work or surveys of others' lab studies.

is the road through which human knowledge itself advances. Whether it is astrophysics, gender studies, American history, or sports medicine, all educational programs will involve some level of research. Some require more than others, but nearly all institutions that are accredited or have any reputation will require heavy research and will have high standards for it.

chapter TWO

Where
to Begin

With a better idea of what research papers entail, the next step is one of the biggest ones: where to begin. In some cases, you will have a limited amount of topics to choose from. This may depend on the class the paper is assigned for and the teacher assigning it. On the other hand, you may have a lot of leeway in what kinds of topics to choose. Some researchers work better with more guidance, others work better with less.

WHAT TO WRITE AND RESEARCH

Let's say you have some leeway in choosing something to research and write about. The first step is to choose a field. Then you need to narrow down and choose a more specific topic or issue within that field. There are benefits to choosing a field and subject you enjoy learning about. It can also be interesting to branch out into one you may be curious about or even one you have no interest in. This last option can help you be truly objective. That is, if you have no biases or any particular opinions about the subject, you may be more open to certain ideas you discover in your research.

Researchers tackling education may pick charter schools or government policies such as No Child Left Behind as possible subjects. History students might be interested in the World War II era and then might zero in on how different types of combat or weapons helped the war efforts of the Americans, Nazi Germans, Soviets, or Japanese, for example.

If you are stumped for a topic or have one but have no clue as to where to begin, online search engines such as Google can be valuable resources.

Google   world war ii   🔍

world war ii
world war iii
world war ii **combatants**
world war ii **dates**

World War II - Wikipedia
https://en.wikipedia.org/wiki/**World_War_II** ▾
World War II also known as the Second World War, was a global war that lasted from 1939 to 1945, although related conflicts began earlier. It involved the vast ...
World War II casualties · Timeline of World War II · India in World War II · Allied

World War II - Battles, Facts, Videos & Pictures - History.com
www.history.com/topics/**world-war-ii** ▾
Coming just two decades after the last great global conflict, the Second **World War** was the most widespread and deadliest **war** in history, involving more than 30 countries and resulting in more than 50 million military and civilian deaths (with some estimates as high as 85 million ...

World War II History - History (history.com)
www.history.com/topics/**world-war-ii**/world-war-ii-history ▾
Find out more about the history of **World War II** History, including videos, interesting articles, pictures, historical features and more. Get all the facts on ...

World War II | HistoryNet

ZEROING IN ON A TOPIC

Once you've narrowed down your top, you need to decide what aspect you will research. You may have expectations about what you will discover in your research. A paper covering World War II in which a writer makes the case that it was better natural resources and manufacturing abilities that helped America win the Pacific conflict over Japan is an example of zeroing in. The same is true for a paper in which one examines how several US states have improved or declined in educational results after opening more charter schools.

Whatever subject you pick or are assigned, there should be a clear idea of what question you are trying to ask and what idea you are trying to get across. The first is a research question. The second is a research thesis.

RESEARCH QUESTION AND THESIS

A good research question should not be too specific, nor too broad or general. You can come up with a good one by doing some general research on a topic. Often, it is enough to do some preliminary online searches and see what is being discussed within the field.

The research thesis can be an answer to the research question, a summary of what you discover in the course of your research, or what you believe you will discover. It may change during the journey of information gathering you embark on. Narrowing down a question will also help narrow down the potentially big list of sources you might use. This might help with that sense of mild panic many students feel when they are just starting a research paper, too!

Thus, if a research question asks, "What are the pros and cons of public school education in the United States for working class youth?," one possible research thesis might be, "Public school education in the United States is unfixable, and alternatives, such as charter schools, should be explored, to properly educate working class youth." A counterpoint thesis might declare, "Public schools are superior

Your sources may help you narrow down your research question. Conversely, your research question may help you narrow down your potential sources.

QUESTIONS TO ASK YOURSELF ABOUT YOUR RESEARCH QUESTION

According to Duke University, there are several questions that can help you formulate, or come up with, research questions. In the humanities (topics such as the English language, literature, religion, history, music, philosophy, etc.), these include:

1) Is the question something I or others care about?
2) Is it arguable?
3) Does the research question provide a new take on an old idea?
4) Does it solve a problem?
5) Is the research question something you can cover in the time allotted and with your resources?
6) What information do you need to answer it?

For the sciences (such as physics, chemistry, and geology) and for subjects lumped under the social sciences (such as sociology and anthropology), statistics and other data will require that you think about the following things when you formulate your research question. In other words, will your research accomplish one of the following four benchmarks?

1) How can you define or measure specific facts or gather

them about a specific phenomenon?
2) How do you combine those facts and theories?
3) How do you compare theories? Models? Hypotheses?
4) How do you prove that a certain research method is more effective than others? Which do you use?

to alternative schools/charter schools and are sufficient to meet the needs of working class youth." You may have heard various opinions matching either of these declarations, but to isolate your own thesis, you need to do the research.

SKILLS TO KEEP IN MIND

As you begin the process of writing your research paper—especially if it is the very first one you are doing—you may find it helpful to examine your strengths and weaknesses when it comes to the major research skills. These include critical reading and critical thinking.

Can you read critically? Getting the main idea of an article or other research paper can sometimes take more than one read-through. Taking notes on the main points and making sure you understand what is being said are important. We do not always get something, or get its true meaning, the first time around.

It can also help to summarize and paraphrase (to rewrite and rephrase the author's ideas with your own

19

words) the work of another person, to help digest it more easily. This helps researchers question and challenge the author's ideas.

Critical thinking means taking in what you have read and weighing the information. This helps you distinguish among opinion pieces, academic content, propaganda (biased or misleading information that benefits a certain party), advertising, and established and reputable sources. It can also mean "reading between the lines" and identifying catchwords that are made to appeal to emotions and that obscure (or hide) the real meaning of what people are saying.

What parts of your reading do you agree with? What parts seem unrealistic or suspicious to you, based on their evidence, and what you have read before? Research involves organization. Important early steps involve organizing others' ideas as well as your own and sifting through to find what seems most valid. With that in mind, ask yourself: can you identify facts when you read a source? Can you tell the difference between a fact and an interpretation?

chapter THREE

Doing
the Research

For simpler projects, such as opinion essays, reading a few articles online can provide background. But writing research papers demands greater depth. Consult as many sources as possible and as wide a variety of them as your topic and research question and thesis require. Learn how to classify sources and how to weigh their importance to fully support your idea or argument.

TYPES OF SOURCES

Sources can be classified according to how close or far removed they are from an actual historical event, era, document, or phenomenon. These can be loosely lumped into primary, secondary, and tertiary sources.

PRIMARY SOURCES

According to Virginia Tech's University Libraries site, for social sciences and humanities topics, primary sources "are the direct evidence for firsthand accounts of events without

Students gaze at documents from the 1961 inauguration of President John F. Kennedy at the John F. Kennedy Museum and Presidential Library, in Boston, Massachusetts. Such items are primary sources.

secondary analysis or interpretation . . . [works] that [were] created or written contemporary with the period or subject being studied." Someone researching the presidential administration of John F. Kennedy, for example, will seek primary sources associated with the man, his aides, and the era, including diaries kept by him and his advisers, a painting he sat for, and similar artifacts. These are original documents that provide firsthand information. Other examples include all original artworks, photographs, speeches, and literary works.

In the sciences, primary sources are defined a bit differently. These include documents that describe original research. A journal article in which scientists first share their findings with the world is an example. Others might be reports of conference proceedings, published lab notebooks, copies of intellectual patents on inventions or processes, and more. Anything presenting original research counts. One limitation, though, is that the ideas and theories may be new and relatively untested and not yet validated by peers trying to replicate the research.

SECONDARY SOURCES

Secondary sources are a step further removed. They comment on or discuss primary sources. Their most notable feature is that they provide interpretation. Thus, while a speech of JFK's is a primary source, an academic article about it is a secondary source. Examples of secondary sources include articles from academic journals, monographs (works on a particular subject or small area of learning), biographies, dissertations (long essays or research papers written in academia), and even indexes, bibliographies, or other accompanying back matter found at the end of books.

The sciences have their own set of secondary sources, such as monographs, review articles (articles that tell the reader about the current stage of knowledge about a subject), and even textbooks. Secondary sources can provide comparisons of different theories still under debate. They also cover historical overviews of how the subject or field has changed over time.

TERTIARY SOURCES

One further step from secondary sources are tertiary sources—"tertiary" meaning third in order or importance. They summarize or condense larger amounts of material from secondary or primary sources and will usually cite these directly. You are familiar with one of the most common: the encyclopedia. Handbooks providing quick reference guides to particular subjects, as well as dictionaries, almanacs, timelines, chronologies, and more, are all tertiary sources.

Tertiary sources are a great way to dive into a new subject you are unfamiliar with, confirm certain points,

Physical copies of encyclopedias such as these are still accessible in many places, but many researchers today are able to access such tertiary sources digitally.

statistics, or other information, and point you in the right direction to actual primary and secondary sources. But they should not be relied on as the backbone of your research. A real research paper needs to go deeper.

KNOWING WHERE TO LOOK

Today, students' natural instinct might be to use free internet resources for research first. Google, Wikipedia, YouTube, and other well-known sites are certainly incredibly valuable and convenient sources. The problem is that many students—even in higher education—use the internet as the first, second, and last stop in their research. If you are creative, you can find much of valuable use via free online searches, including primary sources, when working on a research paper. Search engines, including Google, are the most common access point for this kind of research. Simply enter a search term, and scroll through pages of results. This is a great first step.

ACADEMIC AND RESEARCH DATABASES

However, for reasons this work discusses in several sections, researchers should dig deeper. There is a whole world of information out there to be discovered via your school library, university libraries, and public libraries in your region. While free search engines unlock information, many of the most valuable and useful collections of online, organized information, known as databases, require passwords to access them.

Many databases require subscriptions. While these are too expensive for most people to subscribe to for household use, academic libraries and schools often subscribe to many at once. A school's students or someone with a public library card can then use these free of charge. Library databases are especially useful for students who lack home internet access. They can also use the library's online workstations or its Wi-Fi access.

Whatever you are researching, there is probably a database dedicated to it. Databases also help researchers cut out much of the distracting, irrelevant search results that may come up when searching online.

The following are just a few examples of databases you could use. Consult a teacher or librarian for even more options:

- ARTStor: This database contains more than 1.5 million digital images of artworks.

- JSTOR: More than 7,000 educational institutions use this massive database, which grants access to about 1,500 academic journals, as well as books and primary sources for art, the humanities, and social sciences.

- Access World News: Research Collection: This periodi-

Machines such as this microfiche reader will probably remain useful for quite some time, with billions of records remaining out there to be converted.

cal resource offers more than 500 million news articles from more than 8,000 sources worldwide, dating back to the 1980s.

- Embase: Science and health information is provided via more than 25 million records from 7,600 journals.

- LexisNexis: This is the world's largest resource to look up legal and public records.

- Britannica Library Edition: This is an electronic version of the popular encyclopedia geared toward younger users.

- ProQuest: This company is the creator of extensive general and specialized databases for the sciences, business, career and technical education, criminal justice, education, and many more fields, including those dedicated to different nations and cultures worldwide.

HELP AND TIPS WITH DATABASES

Databases are fairly easy to use, with clear instructions, but what if you think that you need a bit of extra help in getting started? Fear not because there is no shame in asking for help. Even in high school, and especially after, teachers will be happy to explain where and how to access these databases. Librarians will, too. It is their job, after all, to help you with them. Once you find out where and how, you can get cracking at a library computer near you.

A few tips to using databases effectively will help your research go more smoothly. One is to identify the search terms and key concepts that will help you find the best sources.

The way you search for information will have an impact on the quality of your research, too. Avoid casting too wide a wide a net (looking for too much information) or too narrowly focusing on one thing. You may miss important information, either because you have too much to comb through, or too little to give your research much depth.

BOOLEAN OPERATORS

Another friend in your research quest is what is called the Boolean operator. These are simple words you are familiar with: AND, OR, and NOT. They are used as search terms when using library research databases. These operators can help you make combinations to find what you need. "War AND Disease" will return all articles that have both terms within. "War OR disease" will return all hits that have either "war" or "disease," some with both, others with only one of the terms. For example, you can look up "death penalty OR capital punishment." The last operator, NOT, should be used with care because it can eliminate many useful hits. Searching for "European wars NOT World War II" would eliminate the second phrase from the search.

Most databases will have an advanced search option, which can help you find important key phrases, and create search parameters. Someone searching for articles on recent controversies surrounding the antivaccination movement, for instance, could limit their search to the years 2000 to 2016, in articles only in certain journals or periodicals, written by certain authors. Look for particular subject headings, which are assigned to all books and articles in databases by reviewers.

PHYSICAL BOOKS

The convenience of e-books has opened up worlds of information to readers. Many organizations, including major research libraries, are making digital copies of physical books (digitization). Still, it will be a long time before all books are available digitally, online or otherwise. There are millions of books in the world! But only a small fraction of these have been digitized.

The rest exist in library stacks, in private collections, and some even on microfilm, microfiche, and similar formats. Some of the most important books for your project might exist only in hard copy at a library. It may even be a reference edition that cannot be taken out. Librarians, library websites, and physical card catalogs can help you locate them. It is worthwhile to take the time to track down the most useful sources. Unless your assignment is for a quick research project, you should budget enough time to do this kind of research.

chapter FOUR

Organize, Outline, Write, and Edit

While you do research, it pays to be organized. Make sure to take good notes and to classify them properly. If your research paper has several main points, it is necessary to keep your notes in order. This can mean keeping a list of page numbers with the relevant authors and titles of the works you use. Some students find it useful to keep a whole separate notebook for organizing, or to assign certain folders on a laptop, tablet, or other device. Keep folders organized, and write down all the necessary search terms that will help you look up the information later, when you're getting ready to do a first draft.

INTRODUCTION, BODY, AND CONCLUSION

At a very basic level, the body of a research paper has three parts: introduction, body, and conclusion. Keeping to this structure keeps your information well organized and clear.

It helps the writer move logically from one point to the next, instead of just delivering a "data dump," or a collection of points or information with little to connect them.

The introduction may provide some basic context about the topic's importance and your motivation for exploring it. Your research approach is also discussed here. Did you talk to interview subjects? Did you mainly review and compare different ideas to come to your conclusion? How did you use your sources and what kind were they?

Taking good notes is vital since it helps one figure out where sources fit in the general scheme of a research paper.

Most important, the introduction provides the reader with your thesis statement, or argument. What is the main point of your paper?

The body of your paper is where you present the points that support your argument or assertion. One rule many students find useful is the "rule of three." That is, three arguments are ideal for relating your case to readers. Your first should be strong, the next one stronger, and the last the strongest one, to finish on a high note. Finally, your conclusion should summarize all your points and wrap your argument up, showing how you have successfully proved your thesis statement.

WRITING THE PAPER

Beginning can be the hardest part. However, with good notes, an outline, and an objective, a well-planned research paper practically writes itself. Trying to get everything perfect the first time out—on the first draft of the paper—can actually sometimes backfire. Many writers get bogged down in the details. A better strategy is to try and get as much down as possible without overthinking it.

Fixing any problems in a second or third draft is often a better game plan. If there is time, take a break for a day or so, and return to the paper to make revisions. You may be surprised how much insight some time away provides.

After a first draft, make sure to ask yourself the following questions. Does the paper accomplish what the the-

Though it might seem redundant if you have already used your software's spelling and grammar checks, going line by line through your paper for mistakes is always a good idea.

sis statement declares? Are the arguments strong enough? Are they put forward clearly enough? It would be a shame to do extensive, important research on your topic and fail to get your point across to your audience.

PROOFREADING AND FACT-CHECKING

Even if a paper's general structure and arguments are strong, sloppy execution can still sink it. Grammar and consistency are very important. Make sure that facts and figures are consistent throughout a paper. Make sure that there is no change in a research thesis from the introduction through the conclusion. A thorough reading will help determine that.

In addition, making sure that all the numbers line up correctly is crucial. As the saying goes, "the devil is in the details." A paper with many carefully researched charts and statistics can be impressive. But if only a few numbers are off—especially if you did some calculations yourselves—it can ruin your efforts.

DOUBLE- AND TRIPLE-CHECK

Similarly, go through every page and make sure any dates, figures, or other crucial numerical and chronological facts are the same throughout. It would be embarrassing to turn in a paper on the Iraq War in which you say the war began in 2030 (instead of the actual year, 2003).

Even if you have double-checked certain facts during your research, and you are confident of their accuracy, perform a quick internet check of all facts once you have a first or second draft ready. Some details may not be in dispute (for example, the US invasion of Iraq began on March 20, 2003), while others may be, especially among different sources (the number of casualties of the war, for example). Be sure that all the names of places, people, and documents are accurate and spelled correctly. Where there are two or more accepted spellings of a person or thing, try to pick the most common one and make sure it is the same throughout your paper.

SHARPEN YOUR WRITING: STYLE GUIDES AND WRITING MANUALS

It is never too early to try to improve and perfect your research paper writing. Even though using these resources all the time may be several years off in your education, style and writing guides can be useful and provide tips that will give a budding writer more confidence and make your papers feel more professional and formal. Especially in college-level high school coursework, students are expected to learn standardized formatting. Here are some of the guides you will probably be expected to become familiar with. It is never too early to get a head start. You can find these guides in your school and local libraries, borrow them from helpful friends, mentors, and instructors, or maybe even get them as presents on special occasions. All of these have electronic versions, and some even have free chapters available for download.

- The Modern Language Association's *MLA Style Manual and Guide to Scholarly Publishing* is an academic style guide commonly used in the United States, Canada, and among academics worldwide, mainly in the humanities, including English, literature, foreign language studies, philosophy, religion, art, and architecture.

- The *Publication Manual of the American Psychological Association* is the preferred style guide for writing research papers in the social sciences, including political science, law, criminal justice, education, business and economics, communications, and more.

- The *Chicago Manual of Style*, published since 1906 by the University of Chicago Press, is used in American English publishing, and can be applied to research on literature. Closely related is *A Manual for Writers of Research Papers, Theses, and Dissertations*, from the same publisher, also known as the Turabian manual, which provides extra standards for citing sources.

- The Council of Science Editors' *Scientific Style and Format* guide is the preferred guide for writers presenting papers in biology, chemistry, physics, geology, mathematics, health sciences, and other topics related to science, technology, engineering, and math (STEM).

In some cases, you may want to note these differences, while in others, it is better to exclude details that are not essential to your argument. Of course, a true scholar shouldn't hide facts or information that challenges his or her thesis.

Collaborative software, such as Google Docs, allows you to easily store and share research materials from virtually any location.

Whether at home or at the library, keeping a Microsoft Word document or other searchable copy of the paper using a word processing program will help you search easily through it for particular words, phrases, and numbers. Word is often installed on many library or school computers. Other free software programs (freeware) are compatible with most computers. Some of the better-known ones are AbiWord, OpenOffice.org, which has programs equivalent to most Microsoft Office software, and online-hosted ones such as Google Docs.

chapter FIVE

Research Citations and Ethics

For personal essays and other informal writing, it is your own opinions and ideas that you write down. By attaching your name to the essay, you are claiming that the words and ideas within are, to some extent, your own. There is no real need to credit other sources if you, say, pen an op-ed for your school paper entitled "Why I Believe Metal Detectors are Unnecessary in Our School."

But research papers are different, by their very nature. They often rely on multiple sources, sometimes even dozens or hundreds. No matter how minor a point or quotation may be to the big picture, it needs to be credited to the original source. Another term for this is "citation."

PROPER CITATIONS

Citation is one of the most important aspects of research. Without it, no one could tell where writers obtained their information. It is necessary to trace the progress of ideas and to give credit where credit is due. Research is often

If you flip through a meticulously researched work, you will often find pages upon pages of source citations. It's always better to err on the side of citing more than you need rather than not enough.

hard work. It insults the hard work others have done to use their ideas, quotes, or data without crediting them. It is also considered unethical and is one of the behaviors classified as plagiarism. Even accidentally forgetting to cite a work, or improperly citing it, can result in charges of plagiarism against you in high school or at the college and graduate school level.

Punishments for plagiarism can be as mild as having to redo a paper and/or getting a failing grade, to much harsher penalties, such as suspension and even expulsion from schools and degree programs. For some scholars, plagiarism can ruin their careers, even many years after the act itself.

Keeping detailed records of your research is important not only for the content itself, but for the various forms

FORMATTING FOOTNOTES AND ENDNOTES

Each section of your research paper may have its own footnotes or endnotes, numbered callouts where statistics, quotes, and other information appear within the text. They may provide an extra bit of text for context. They also usually refer to a specific set of pages where the information appears in the original source. When these citations appear at the bottom of a page of a research paper, they are footnotes. When collected after the main body of the paper, they are endnotes. Some teachers recommend choosing endnotes instead of footnotes to allow for cleaner-looking pages.

At the end of your paper, you may have a reference list or bibliography. This should list all the sources you used in a particular order, usually alphabetical according to the author, or the organization, publication, or website, if an author is not citable. These can include books, collections, journal articles, periodicals, and websites of all kinds, including reference sites, online handbooks, government websites, and many other sources.

After a first reference of a work, a footnote will usually have a shortened version of the author list, referencing only the first name in the series. When two footnotes from the same work follow one another, the second can be shortened to "ibid" (Latin for "in the same place"), with a page number provided if the footnote is derived from a different part of the same book or article.

of citations that you may use in your paper. A good idea is to open a new file or new section of a notebook for every source you use so you do not mix up where you are drawing from.

THE PITFALLS OF RESEARCHING ONLINE

Another reason to go the extra mile to obtain actual books and access primary sources via research databases is that online searches can lead in many, sometimes confusing, directions. You may come across what looks like great new insights on a topic, on a more or less professional-looking website. You then realize there are few or no citations for what seem to be some great quotes, and you can't really tell where the author's ideas have come from. How can you trust the information?

Or you may waste time searching through misinformation or biased content. Many seemingly respectable sources online are actually promoting an agenda, rather than providing impartial, objective scholarship. Even established news organizations are occasionally dead wrong about something, before issuing later corrections.

GENERAL RESEARCH ETHICS

As discussed, plagiarism is dishonest, unethical, and has serious consequences. Truly being able to get away with it these days, with the ease of plagiarism checker programs that professors or teaching assistants have at their finger-tips, may actually prove to be more trouble than actually doing the work honestly.

Students can also end up plagiarizing unintentionally. When you do not consistently take notes and credit your sources as you read through book after book and visit multiple destinations online, the large amount of material can become something of a blur. You may write down a phrase or series of passages, thinking them original, and that you were inspired out of the blue. It later turns out you repeated something verbatim from another source without realizing it. This kind of mistake is easier to make than you think.

Plagiarism has been a controversial and concerning topic for educators, especially in the last two decades, since the internet has made it so easy and tempting for some students to cut corners. Some justify it because of the great pressure many pupils are under nowadays and do not plagiarize lightly, while others are more casual about it.

DOING YOUR OWN WORK

Businesses and individuals that promise "research help" for a fee have partly enabled plagiarism and cheating. These parties, sometimes known as essay or term paper "mills" advertise online, as well as on campuses and via word of mouth. Many claim that they only assist students to do their work. In actuality, they sell prewritten or made-to-order research papers. It can be enticing for students, par-

If work is piling up and a deadline is looming, even a good, normally conscientious student may be tempted to take shortcuts. Resist this temptation, however.

ticularly the many who feel overworked to begin with, to skip dozens of hours of research and get a decent grade with zero effort.

However, as much of a cliché as the old saying is, students who cheat on research papers are truly only cheating themselves. They simultaneously throw away the opportunity to sharpen their skills, obtain an unfair advantage over their fellow students who complete their papers honestly, and cheat themselves out of an education. With the risk to one's reputation and school career so great, it is truly a foolish risk. Writing a paper for a friend or having one do it for you is also unethical.

Research into Your Future

S tudents have plenty of opportunities to dip their feet into academic research as they move through their academic careers. Starting early can help you become a seasoned researcher by the time you are a senior in high school or starting college.

The amount of information in our hyperconnected world may seem overwhelming. Scholars of earlier eras perhaps had a more straightforward path in writing research papers. But do not underestimate the incredible opportunities current and emerging technologies will provide.

RESEARCH IN THE TECH ERA

Students nowadays may be entering a golden age of convenience and ease of research because of technology. To access important and rare sources, scholars once had to travel great distances to read or view primary sources up close. For a copy of a speech from a professor speaking about a topic relevant to a research paper, one sometimes had to wait a long time for it to be transcribed and printed in a journal or a book.

Today, many universities and organizations live-stream speeches, conferences, and other important events. Such gatherings can be accessed easily afterward on their websites or might be uploaded to YouTube. If there is one thing technology has improved, it is access to certain kinds of information and content. Of course, much of the most sought-after and relevant video and audio content may require subscriptions or one-time purchase fees. But there are plenty of materials that schools and individual academics offer for free.

The trick for scholars just learning the ropes now is to maintain a certain level of academic rigor, or standards, with the new tools at your disposal. As discussed earlier, the danger is becoming too complacent, or comfortable. This can lead to taking shortcuts and letting the quality of research suffer.

SUPER SOFTWARE

Software for all kinds of electronic devices—from laptop computers to tablets to smartphones—will make much of the tedious and time-consuming work involved in research a bit easier. Even now, students and teachers alike can leverage new software. There's even software for scanning documents of all kinds with a smartphone and converting them into text. While such processes can still be riddled with errors, they are being constantly improved.

The internet can connect you with professors teaching online classes or allow you to contact interview subjects easily.

TO WIKIPEDIA . . . OR NOT?

One ongoing dilemma among many teachers (and students) is the status of Wikipedia as a tertiary source for research. The online encyclopedia with many thousands of articles in dozens of languages can be a valuable resource.

But many teachers still discourage using it as anything other than a mere starting point. One strategy is to use Wikipedia to collect keywords and ideas and to begin your research in earnest from there. Many of the website's articles have dozens of articles referenced at the end, as well as links to relevant web resources.

(continued on the next page)

(continued from the previous page)

Students should not use Wikipedia as their sole source for projects. Wikipedia has come a long way from its early days, when its information was often inaccurate, and is slowly gaining more approval from academia. Its accuracy on many subjects has been found by some studies to be not far off from more highly vetted sources like Encyclopedia Britannica. One of its main benefits and the reason it can stay free is that volunteers update and edit its articles constantly. Many of them are experts in their fields. It is also a drawback because it can be easy to overlook misinformation and mistakes. Also, a few bad apples occasionally intentionally sabotage articles for their own ends or act as internet trolls.

In the future, many real-time functions, such as cross-referencing other more respected databases and computer-enabled fact-checking, could make Wikipedia and similar sites even more attractive for scholars of all levels of expertise.

Software such as Adobe Acrobat allows someone to highlight text in a PDF document and type up notes, much like a student jotting down notes in the margin of a book or printout of a paper. Not long from now, students will be able to easily use programs to convert spoken word into text notes in documents. Other apps might automatically convert the identifying information from a book's cover and interior—title, author names, publication date, and even selected pages—into footnotes or endnotes or bibliographical formats. Other scholars have envisioned electronic readers that "look" through entire books (both physical and e-books) for a researcher. These may take students to the relevant sections or even summarize and interpret books more quickly.

COLLECTING DATA QUICKLY

In the sciences and social sciences new time-saving programs that help collect and analyze various data are even more valuable, arguably, than in the humanities. *Wired* magazine reported recently on collecting surveys of thousands of employees for business management research and how new techniques had revolutionized such work:

Image-to-text apps for smartphones and other electronic devices, which use optical character recognition (OCR), are just one of the technologies that may make research even easier.

"In the past . . . a study like this required printing

thousands of surveys, buying stamped envelopes, and hoping everyone receiving the questionnaire would complete it and mail it back. It would also require a major time investment from the organization being surveyed. Conducting experimental research would be even more complicated, requiring busy research aides to print and organize countless scenarios."

The modern online study has saved researchers countless hours of work. Now it is necessary only to email hundreds of recipients or conduct the study on social media networks. Collection of and even a limited analysis of the data is automated. A single person can do the job once done by several researchers and assistants, for a tiny fraction of the cost. Or an ad can be posted on social media or a classified advertisements website seeking people who match certain criteria to answer an online questionnaire. The researcher need not even devise a questionnaire online but can enlist the services of a specialized site for it.

STAYING SHARP

Even in this day and age, when it has become so much easier to collect data and do research, it is still important for students to learn the necessary skills involved in writing research papers. Software is not perfect yet, and it will be a long time before much of the work in research is completely automated. And the intellectual effort to find and digest new knowledge is often as important as finding the right information to begin with. Technological "fixes" can sometimes rob research of the excitement and joy that many students discover in it. Excitedly reading a great book with amazing new insights can be far superior to having an app spit out its main points. For now, it remains up in the air what the future holds for technology's effects on scholarship and research.

Research should be done for its own sake, not just for a grade. Learning and discovery can inspire you throughout your life.

SKILLS FOR A LIFETIME

Take it slowly if you need to when learning the ins and outs of research papers. The skills of organization, seeking sources, note taking, outlining, and writing come more easily to some and take more work for others. With patience, time, and practice, anyone can become an expert researcher. By doing so, they gain a skill set that transfers not only to the academic world but is applicable to many professional settings.

Research is the heavy lifting that was done to figure out the physics involved that helped humanity build jet engines, get to the moon, and cure all manner of diseases. It is the work that is involved in many of the new ideas that governments have for how to help their nations and their peoples. It also helps us understand ourselves and how individuals and their societies really work.

Pretty much every industry or academic discipline that you may want to be a part of later in life relies on research. A state government official in charge of schools figuring out what kinds of classroom techniques will best help young learners and a scientist assigned to figure the most effective way to design safe airplane engines can both do their jobs much better with the best new information and ideas possible. With finely tuned research skills, you will be ready to add much to your classroom learning environments, your chosen academic field, your workplaces and employers, and to society at large.

GLOSSARY

BIAS An unfair or unfounded preference for something or dislike of another.

BOOLEAN OPERATORS Words used to help researchers narrow down information in searches of academic databases.

CITATION The process of officially crediting sources within one's own research.

DATABASE A structured collection of academic data accessible via users' tailored, coordinated searches.

DISCIPLINE A branch of human knowledge.

ESSAY MILL A company or individual that sells students academic content that the customer hopes unethically to pass off as his or her own original work.

HUMANITIES Academic disciplines that study human culture, including language, philosophy, religion, the arts, music, and more.

NGO Short for "nongovernmental organization," an NGO is a nonprofit organization that is independent from states and governmental organizations. Many NGOs are charities that rely on donations and volunteer help.

OBSCURE To conceal or hide something from being seen.

PERSUASIVE ESSAY An essay that presents an opinion about an issue or topic, written with the aim of persuading the reader of the rightness of that opinion.

PLAGIARISM Copying ideas or verbatim text from other scholars or sources and attempting to pass it off as your own; sometimes this can be done accidentally.

PRIMARY SOURCE An original document, artwork, record, or artifact that provides firsthand information about a subject or topic.

SECONDARY SOURCE A source that interprets or provides secondhand information about primary sources or subjects.

SOCIAL SCIENCES Academic disciplines that concern themselves with society and the relationships among people, including economics, political science, and sociology, among others.

FOR MORE INFORMATION

American Library Association
50 East Huron Street
Chicago, IL 60611
(800) 545-2433
Website: http://www.ala.org
The American Library Association is a professional organization uniting thousands of school librarians and
libraries throughout the United States. Its mission is
to promote libraries and library education.

Association of Research Libraries
21 Dupont Circle NW, Suite 800
Washington, DC 20036
(201) 296-2296
Website: http://www.arl.org
The Association of Research Libraries is a nonprofit organization uniting the leading research libraries in the
United States and Canada, with the aim of coordi-
nating action to promote scholarship and research
within North America generally, including legislation
and lobbying.

Canadian Association of Research Libraries (CARL)
309 Cooper Street, Suite 203
Ottawa, ON K2P 0G5
Canada
(613) 482-9344
Website: http://www.carl-abrc.ca

The Canadian Association of Research Libraries (CARL) helps develop and deploy research data management initiatives, promotes scholarly communications, and encourages the role of research libraries in publishing and academic advancement.

Library of Congress
101 Independence Avenue SE
Washington, DC 20540-1400
(202) 707-9779
Website: https://www.loc.gov
The Library of Congress serves as the research center for the US Congress and as a repository, cataloger, and archive for much of the published output of both the United States and the world at large. It is the largest library in the world and provides access to thousands of primary source artifacts.

National Archives and Records Administration
8601 Adelphi Road
College Park, MD 20740-6001
(866) 272-6272
Website: http://www.archives.govThe National Archives and Records Administration collects and manages important documents having to do with the operations of the US federal government.

Natural Resources Canada: The Atlas of Canada
615 Booth Street, Room 650
Ottawa, ON K1A 0E9
Canada
(613) 995-0947
Website: http://www.nrcan.gc.ca/earth-sciences/geography/
atlas-canada
The Atlas of Canada, administered by Natural Resources
    Canada, is the official mapmaker of Canada. The
    online interactive edition documents Canada's land-
    scape and demographics with easily accessible data.

WEBSITES

Because of the changing nature of internet links, Rosen
Publishing has developed an online list of websites related
to the subject of this book. This site is updated regularly.
Please use this link to access the list:

http://www.rosenlinks.com/SFS/research

FOR FURTHER READING

Bell, Suzanne S. *Librarian's Guide to Online Searching: Cultivating Database Skills for Research and Instruction.* 4th ed. Santa Barbara, CA: Libraries Unlimited, 2015.

Booth, Wayne C., Gregory G. Colomb, and Joseph M. Williams. *The Craft of Research.* 3rd ed. Chicago, IL: University of Chicago Press, 2008.

Hacker, Diana, and Nancy Sommers. *Rules for Writers.* 7th ed. New York, NY: Bedford/St. Martin's Press, 2011.

Lester, James D., and James D. Lester, Jr. *Writing Research Papers: A Complete Guide.* 15th ed. Upper Saddle River, NJ: Pearson, 2014.

Lindeen, Mary. *Smart Online Searching: Doing Digital Research.* Minneapolis, MN: Lerner Publishing, 2016.

Mann, Thomas. *The Oxford Guide to Library Research.* 4th ed. New York, NY: Oxford University Press, 2015.

Marcovitz, Hal. *Online Information and Research.* San Diego, CA: Referencepoint Press, 2012.

Reinking, James A. *Strategies for Successful Writing: A Rhetoric, Research Guide, Reader, and Handbook.* 10th ed. Upper Saddle River, NJ: Prentice Hall, 2014.

Porterfield, Jason. *Conducting Basic and Advanced Searches.* New York, NY: Rosen Publishing, 2011.

Toronto Public Library. *The Research Virtuoso: How to Find Anything You Need to Know.* Toronto, ON: Annick Press, 2012.

BIBLIOGRAPHY

Abbott, Alana Joli. "Tools for College Students: Learning the New MLA Guidelines." Cengage Learning. September 30, 2016. http://blog.cengage.com/tools-college-students-learning-new-mla-guidelines.

American Library Association. "Using Primary Sources." Retrieved November 7, 2016. http://www.ala.org/rusa/sections/history/resources/pubs/usingprimary-sources.

Cooper, Diane. "How to Write an Original Research Paper (and Get It Published)." National Center for Biotechnology Information. April 2015. https://www.ncbi.nlm.nih.gov/pmc/articles/PMC4404856.

ESC Online Writing Center. "What is a Research Paper?" SUNY Empire State College. Retrieved October 1, 2016. https://www.esc.edu/online-writing-center/resources/research/research-paper.

Gardiner, Eileen, and Ronald G. Musto. *The Digital Humanities: A Primer for Students and Scholars*. New York, NY: Cambridge University Press, 2015.

Gibaldi, Phyllis Franklin. *MLA Handbook for Writers of Research Papers*. 7th ed. New York, NY: Modern Language Association, 2009.

Goshert, John Charles. *Entering the Academic Conversation: Strategies for Research Writing*. Upper Saddle River, NJ: Pearson, 2014.

Herrera, Jack. "Viewpoint: Essay Mills are Tempting, But Also Sickening." *USA Today* College. August 23, 2016.

http://college.usatoday.com/2016/08/23/viewpoint-essay-mills-are-tempting-but-also-sickening.

Massey, Taylor. "Writing a Research Paper: Nine Tips for Student Success." Cengage Learning. September 26, 2014. http://blog.cengage.com/writing-a-research-paper-nine-tips-for-student-success.

Modern Language Association of America. *MLA Handbook.* 8th ed. New York, NY: Modern Language Association, 2016.

Schlein, Alan. *Find It Online: The Complete Guide to Online Research.* 4th ed. Tempe, AZ: Facts on Demand Press, 2014.

Smith, Ryan. "How Technology Is Changing Academic Research." *Wired*, July 2013. https://www.wired.com/insights/2013/07/how-technology-is-changing-academic-research.

Strang, Tami. "Encouraging Students to Use Research Databases." Cengage Learning. October 6, 2015. http://blog.cengage.com/encouraging-students-to-use-research-databases.

Taparia, Neal. "Do Your Research, Cite Sources to be an Effective Writer." *Forbes*, September 23, 2015. http://www.forbes.com.

Turabian, Kate, Wayne C. Booth, and University of Chicago Press Staff. *A Manual for Writers of Research Papers, Theses, and Dissertations: Chicago Style for Students and Researchers.* Rev. ed. Chicago, IL: University of Chicago Press, 2011.

INDEX

A

AbiWord, 38
Access World News, 26–27
Adobe Acrobat, 48
appeal to emotions, 20
ARTStor, 26

B

bias, 14, 20, 42
body, of a paper, 31–33
Boolean operators, 29
Britannica Library Edition, 27

C

Chicago Manual of Style, 37
citations, how to properly
    create for sources,
    39–40, 42
conclusion, of a paper, 31, 33
critical reading skills, 19, 20
critical thinking skills, 19, 20

D

databases, 42, 48
    tips for using, 28–29
    types of, 25–28
drafts, 33–34

E

Embase, 27
encyclopedias, 24, 27, 47–48
endnotes, how to format, 41

F

fact-checking, 35
facts, compared to interpreta-
    tion, 20
footnotes, how to format, 41
freeware, 38

G

Google Docs, 38
Google search engine, 25, 26

H

humanities, 18, 21, 26, 36, 49
Human Rights Watch, 9

I

interpretation, compared to
    facts, 20
introduction, of a paper, 31,
    32–33

J

JSTOR, 26

L

LexisNexis, 27

M

Manual for Writers of Research Papers, Theses, and Dissertations, A, 37
Microsoft Word, 38
MLA Style Manual and Guide to Scholarly Publishing, 36

N

nongovernmental organization (NGO), 9

O

online searches, and determining reputable sources, 42
OpenOffice, 38
opinion essays, 10, 21
outline, 33

P

paper mills, 43–44
persuasive essay, 10
plagiarism, 6, 40, 42–43
portable document format (PDF), 48
primary source, 21–23, 25, 26, 42, 45
printed works, tips for searching, 30
proofreading, 34–35
ProQuest, 28
Publication Manual of the American Psychological Association, 37

R

reading between the lines, 20
research ethics, general rules, 42–43
research papers
   compared to opinion or persuasive essays, 10–11
   experts as sources, 9
   importance of to higher education, 11, 13
   structure of, 31–33
   what they are, 7–9

research questions
  how to formulate one,
    16–17
  questions to help deter-
    mine, 18–19

S

Scientific Style and Format, 37
search engines, 25
secondary source, 21, 23, 24, 25
social sciences, 18, 21, 26, 37, 49
software, 46, 48–49
sources, types of, 21–25
style guides, types of, 36–37
survey of information, 12

T

technology, information
    access and, 45–46
tertiary source, 21, 24–25, 47
thesis, how to formulate one,
    16–17
topics
  choosing, 14–15
  narrowing your focus, 16

W

Wikipedia, 25, 47–48

World Health Organization, 9
writing guides, types of,
    36–37

Y

YouTube, 25

ABOUT THE AUTHOR

Philip Wolny is an editor and author from Queens, New York. He has written multiple titles for Rosen Publishing covering youth-centered topics such as self-help, entrepreneurship, health and hygiene, and academic research and scholarship.

PHOTO CREDITS